To: _____

From: _____

Other books by Gregory E. Lang:

Why a Daughter Needs a Dad
Why a Son Needs a Dad
Why I Love Grandma
Why I Love Grandpa
Why a Son Needs a Mom
Why a Daughter Needs a Mom
Why I Love You

WHY I CHOSE YOU

100 Reasons Why Adopting You Made Us a Family

GREGORY E. LANG

with photographs by Gregory E. Lang
and Janet Lankford-Moran

Cumberland House
Nashville, Tennessee

Cover design: Unlikely Suburban Design
Text design: Lisa Taylor
Photographs: Gregory E. Lang and Janet Lankford-Moran
Cover photo: Gregory E. Lang

Printed in the United States of America
2 3 4 5 6 7 8 — 08 07 06 05 04

To the men and women who opened their hearts and
homes in order to give a child a loving family.

Introduction

As I have worked on my previous seven books I have been blessed with the opportunity to get to know many wonderful families. I have had the pleasure of spending time with gleeful newlyweds, couples in their fifth decade of marriage, couples expecting their first child, couples with as many as eight children, families brought together by remarriage, and families that grew from the decision to take in children who did not have a home to call their own. It is the latter, families that were put together either in part or in whole by adoption, that is celebrated in this book. We recognize their generosity of heart and willingness to accept the unknown, praise the decision to take the often drawn out and tedious steps of adoption, and honor the unquestionable capacity to instantly love someone not of their flesh and blood and give a child a family.

Raising a child is not a right, but a priceless gift. It matters not from where the gift comes, but simply that it is received. There can be absolutely no question that adopting parents are *choosing* to have a child when they adopt, choosing to open their arms and accept the precious gift that was meant just for them. It is this act that makes adoption different from having a child naturally. Clearly, many people who have babies choose to do so, but undeniably, some don't. However, one thing adopted children know for certain is that they were wanted and sought after by their parents. And as they grow up and become aware of the obstacles their parents had to overcome to get them, they realize even more what a blessing it is that they did so.

Whether a domestic or international adoption, an infant or adolescent, a perfectly healthy or a special-needs child, there is, I think, one thing that holds true for all adopted children—that there was once a void in their lives that needed filling. And whether a husband and wife, a single mom, a childless couple or one with a houseful of children, there is also one thing that holds true for all adopting parents—that upon witnessing that void, there came an unquenchable desire to fill it. I know this to be true because I have seen it for myself. I know a woman who by chance learned of a child on the other side of the world who suffered from a medical condition that the woman was knowledgeable about, and now a healthy, happy child lives in the care of her and her husband. I know a couple who learned of a newborn left in a park nestled in a shoebox. They immediately took the necessary steps to become foster parents for that child and are now finalizing the adoption. I know a couple who has adopted several children that require special attention and support. They did so because they believe their lives have been richly blessed by giving to children whose needs are beyond the reach of most. I know many other families with similar heart-moving stories, all of which have the same ending—a family grew larger and happier, a child was loved unconditionally, and good memories were made.

When I asked the people who posed for this book why they chose to adopt, I received many, varied answers. The ones I will never forget are: "I wanted to give someone the wings and freedom to find whatever they may need in life." "Every child should have a family, and I had one to give," and "Parenting is the best destination for those of us that always seem to be searching." These phrases not only helped me think of the one hundred reasons of this book, but also reminded me of why I love my child so much and how very important being a parent is to me. It is the role I value above all others, one that I wanted desperately for years before it became true for me. That is when I felt deeply connected to the people I had met and realized that these families are not so different, after all.

In the end, there are abundant reasons for seeking a child through adoption. Many adoptive parents desperately want children but are unable to have them, or are so fulfilled in the role of parent that they simply want more than the biological children they already have. The adoption process provides these parents with a child who needs parental love and nurturing as much as the parents need the child. In either case, adoptive parents see a need and are led to provide stable homes for children who will flourish because of the love and affection they receive.

It is that choice to give love and affection to a child, that choice to build a family by adoption, that is celebrated within these pages. *Why I Chose You* is about people who had enough love in their hearts that they chose to open their home to someone who needed a family. It's about men and women who, with purposeful intent, said, "You are now a part of this family, my darling, wonderful child. You are and you always will be the choice of my heart. Welcome home."

WHY I CHOSE YOU

I chose you

because I wanted the extra love that you
would bring to my family.

I chose you

to fill my days with a more meaningful purpose.

I chose you

because I wanted the pleasure of watching you grow up.

I chose you . . .

to help me fulfill my potential.

to help me experience all that life has to offer.

to help make the holidays more festive for all.

so that I could teach you all of life's little secrets.

I chose you

to teach me how to play again.

I chose you

because you are the child of my dreams.

I chose you . . .

because I was led to you.

because you needed a loving family, and mine needed you.

because I felt your heart beat when I first held you.

because I wanted to be the one to set an example for you.

I chose you

because I believe every child should have a loving family.

I chose you

because you were and always will be the choice of my heart.

I chose you . . .

because I have always dreamt of being a parent.

because you needed the love that I had to give.

because your heart called out to mine.

because I love giving my heart to someone special.

I chose you

because the love of family is meant to be shared.

I chose you

because I believe that my path always pointed toward you.

I chose you

to teach me new traditions.

I chose you

because I wasn't ready to stop raising children.

I chose you

because my heart longed for a child
to depend on me.

I chose you

because I believed that we would be stronger
together than apart.

I chose you . . .

because I was drawn to your adventurous spirit.

because I was smitten by the sparkle in your eyes.

because I knew that you would love the toys
I had collected for you.

because I wanted to take care of you, as I knew that I could.

I chose you

because I wanted to be the one to encourage
your interests and talents.

I chose you

because I wanted even more than what nature
had in store for me.

I chose you

to bring happiness to the empty places in my heart.

I chose you

because I wanted to be the one to teach you
what you need to know.

I chose you . . .

so that I could sing lullabies once more.

because I wanted to be the one you would turn to
for love and reassurance.

because your little voice spoke to me.

so that I could celebrate your birthday with you.

I chose you

to complete my family.

I chose you

to keep me young at heart.

I chose you

to carry on my family name.

I chose you . . .

when I realized the kind of love I was missing—
that between a parent and a child.

because I needed you to become whole.

because I wanted to help you become an adult.

because I wanted to receive the love you had to give.

I chose you

because my house was longing for children.

I chose you

because I wanted to be the one to show you
a love without limits.

I chose you . . .

because I wanted to do for someone what
my parents did for me.

because I wanted to be the one to care for you when you are sick.

because I wanted to be the confidant you would one day turn to.

because I also want to be a grandparent one day.

I chose you

to add new joy to my life.

I chose you

because you needed a strong heart to guide you.

I chose you

because being a parent is what I enjoy most.

I chose you . . .

to watch the stars with me.

to help me not to overlook the simple but meaningful things.

to explore the wonders of the world with me.

to keep me on my toes.

I chose you

at the moment that I first learned about you.

I chose you

because I wanted to be the one to put
a smile on your face.

I chose you

because I wanted to hold your little hand.

I chose you

to look out for me when I am unable
to do so for myself.

I chose you

because I could see that you had enough love
in your heart for all of us.

I chose you

because I wanted to be the one you'll remember
when you look back on your life.

I chose you . . .

because I love the sound of little feet running across the floor.

because I wanted to be the one you call out to when you are afraid.

when I saw that you were waiting for someone
to hold you close to their heart.

because when I first touched you, I wanted to hold you forever.

I chose you

because I loved the warmth of your smile.

I chose you

to fill my arms, which ached to hold a child.

I chose you

because I wanted to see the world
through the eyes of a child.

I chose you . . .

because I wanted to be the one to show you the warmth of family.

to share a wonderful life with me.

because I wanted to share with you the blessings
that I have received.

because your little voice was sweet music to my ears.

I chose you

because I needed someone to rekindle my imagination.

I chose you

because I felt that we were meant to be together.

I chose you

to fill my house with laughter.

I chose you . . .

because I knew that you would love me
as much as I now love you.

to make family vacations all the more enjoyable.

because I wanted to be the one you would reach for
when you need a hug.

because I wanted to be the one to wipe away your tears.

I chose you

to help make me the best person I could become.

I chose you . . .

to comfort me in my times of need.

so I could shower you with affection.

because I wanted to be the one to "kiss it and make it all better."

because I wanted to make sure that your heart was
prepared for your own child one day.

I chose you

because I wanted to be the one to give you piggyback rides.

I chose you

to pass on to you what I have learned.

I chose you

because I knew we would have lots of fun together.

I chose you . . .

to return with me to all the fun places my parents once took me.

so that we could, in turn, be helpful to others.

because I wanted to give someone special the keepsakes I have saved.

because I wanted to be there for you when you experience life's challenges.

I chose you

because you needed someone, as did I.

I chose you . . .

to carry on my family traditions.

because you touched my heart.

because I wanted to be the one to teach you
how to tie your shoes.

so that neither of us would be alone.

I chose you

to give you the opportunities that were
once given to me.